D0917909

Sports Illustrated

SWIMMING
AND DIVING

The Sports Illustrated Library

BOOKS ON TEAM SPORTS

Baseball	Football: Defense	Ice Hockey
Basketball	Football: Offense	Pitching
Curling: Techniques	Football: Quarterback	Soccer
and Strategy		Volleyball

BOOKS ON INDIVIDUAL SPORTS

Badminton	Horseback Riding	Table Tennis
Fly Fishing	Judo	Tennis
Golf	Skiing	Track: Running Events
Handball	Squash	Track: Field Events

BOOKS ON WATER SPORTS

Powerboating	Small Boat Sailing
Skin Diving and Snorkeling	Swimming and Diving

SPECIAL BOOKS

Dog Training	Training with Weights
Safe Driving	

Sports Illustrated
SWIMMING AND DIVING

**By the Editors of
Sports Illustrated**

**Illustrations
by Harry Schaare
and Ed Vebell**

J. B. LIPPINCOTT COMPANY
Philadelphia and New York

U.S. Library of Congress Cataloging in Publication Data

Main entry under title:

Sports illustrated swimming and diving.

(The Sports illustrated library)
First published in 1961 as two separate works under titles: Sports illustrated book of swimming and Sports illustrated book of diving.
1. Swimming.   2. Diving.   I. Sports illustrated (Chicago).
GV837.S823 1973   797.2   73–8714
ISBN–0–397–01002–8
ISBN–0–397–01003–6 (pbk.)

Cover photograph: Tony Triolo

Photographs on pages 10 and 41: Heinz Kluetmeier

Photograph on page 50: Neil Leifer

Contents

Foreword

Since swimming is best learned at a young age with the help of a knowledgeable instructor, Part 1 of this book is addressed to the parent who plans to teach his child to swim. It was written by the late Matt Mann, coach of the University of Michigan and U.S. Olympic swimming teams, who was renowned for his ability to develop outstanding young swimmers.

Basic diving, on the other hand, can easily be self-taught, and therefore Part 2 is oriented toward the aspiring diver. It was written by former Ohio State and Olympic diving coach Mike Peppe, with the help of Coles Phinizy, *Sports Illustrated* Senior Editor, who also collaborated with Matt Mann on Part 1.

Sports Illustrated
SWIMMING AND DIVING

Part 1
Swimming

THE TEACHER

One need not be a Mark Spitz to get a lot out of swimming. It is more than just fun in the water; it is perhaps the best all-round exercise, using nearly every muscle in the body. In this era of sedentary executives and immobilized television watchers, swimming offers probably the most enjoyable way to retain minimal muscle tone and keep the cardiovascular system in decent repair.

As with any sport, it is best to start young. The age bracket of five to nine years is the preferred time for learning to swim. And the crawl is the stroke that every child should learn first, since it is the most efficient, the best combination of speed and ease in the water.

Anyone who plans to teach a child to swim must first be sure that he himself is at ease in the water. There are parents who, by way of introduction, carry their child into the water while telling him, "Don't be afraid." This is not the way. You can't beat fear out with a drum. As the teacher, you must always be on guard against fear, but this is your exclusive concern; don't share it with your young beginner. When you first lead a child into the water, talk to him about anything under the sun. Keep the project casual, and you will keep him relaxed.

When you teach, do not hurry. The ability of the child after a few weeks, to beat all the neighborhood kids in a short thrash across the pool is no measure of success. Speed in the water lies well beyond the primary aim of easy swimming.

Before they ever try to swim, many children have frolicked in the water, ducked their heads of their own accord and in any number of ways introduced themselves to the new element. Before the child is put through any of the motions of swimming, he should be at ease and used to the feel of water surrounding the body.

The best site for teaching is a lake or bay that affords a gradually sloping, safe bottom. A swimming pool with a bottom sloping gradually from the shallow end is about as good, and a pool five feet deep in the shallow end—roughly up to the teacher's shoulders—will do. Warm water of 80 degrees is more conducive to relaxation than the 70-degree water that most of us find more refreshing. If the water is cold, shorten the lessons to avoid the tension the cold might cause.

Begin by taking the youngster by the hand and wading casually out from the shore. Depending on his reaction, this can be done once or a dozen times, until he is at ease in water up to his waist. Another familiarization method is to have the child kneel in foot-deep water near shore, lean over and put his hands on the bottom while slowly lowering himself to a prone position. This will enable him to walk around on his hands, trailing his legs or kicking them gently. All this is done not so much to give the child any idea of the lift the water affords, or to teach him the kick, as simply to get him used to the feel of the water.

At a pool, where there is no foot-deep water, seat the child on the side with his legs dangling in the water. Have him leave his feet limp and move them alternately up and down by a slight bending of the knees. This will give the neophyte a brief introduction to the idea of the kick.

The beginner may now be taken into water that is shoulder-high and well over his head. Cradling him in his arms, the teacher should walk gradually back and forth while the child kicks his feet idly and loosely. Virtually all instruction is done in water of this depth so that the teacher is on a level with his charge and able to support him without bending over. It is important that both be relaxed. The teacher's sense of touch is an important guide to the beginner's progress, since it is in this way that any tension can be detected. As the child gradually becomes accustomed to having his feet off the bottom, he trusts the teacher and comes to find that the water is a pleasant place. Now the stage has been set for the real business of learning to swim.

THE CRAWL

Kick

Good crawl swimming is essentially a harmony of three diverse actions: (1) the kick, (2) the arm stroke and (3) the breathing. Most instructors begin with the kick, subsequently adding to it the arm stroke and then the breathing.

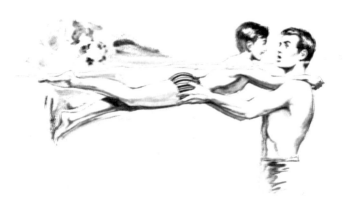

While the teacher holds the beginner in water about chest-high, the child places one hand on either side of the back of the instructor's neck. The teacher then slips his hands around to the front of the child's hips and gently presses up, thus allowing the child to lie prone in the water.

The crawl kick is basically an alternating action of the legs that emanates from the hips. As one leg is lifting up in a vertical plane, the other is dropping down. The feet should be limp, the legs fairly straight but the knees relaxed so that each knee flexes slightly and naturally as the leg finishes the swing upward. Above all, encourage the child to take it

15

easy. The kick should not be fast, and there should not be a shower of spray, but only a ruffling of the surface, with the heel or, at most, the back half of the foot breaking the water.

On the downbeat, the feet should not go deep—no more than nine inches. *The kick must be practiced until it is virtually automatic,* so that when the child starts using his arms, he will continue kicking correctly without giving his legs a thought.

Error one: bending knee too much.

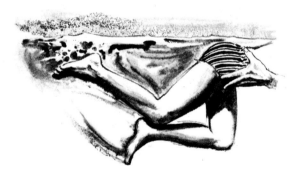

Error two: bicycling the legs.

There are two errors—purposely exaggerated in the illustrations—that beginners are apt to commit when they first try kicking. Many tend to bend the knee too much, so that

the whole foot and part of the leg emerge from the water
on one beat and slap back into the water on the next. To
correct this, the child should stiffen the knee and kick less
vigorously.

Another error is to flex each knee through the downbeat
at the same time thrusting the thigh forward excessively, so
that the leg, rather than swinging up and down, is pumping
back and forth in a pistonlike action. This is called "bicycling" and is corrected by the child's concentration on
stretching the legs back, trying to keep the whole body,
toes to head, in a horizontal plane while kicking.

When a beginning swimmer kicks correctly, the teacher
will feel the gentle thrust and should yield to it by backing
up so that the child progresses slowly through the water.
Sometimes the kick looks good, but there is little or no
thrust. Don't worry about it. Propulsion is only secondary.
The greatest values of the kick, for beginners particularly,
are the lift it affords to the lower, heavier half of the body
and the stability it offers for the whole body.

When the child has acquired reasonable competence in
kicking, place a small, inflated tube around his waist. A
small, cheap tube will do, but it should not buoy up the

youngster unnaturally high. The tube now, rather than the teacher's hands, will give the child support in mid-body. At first, while the learner practices kicking with the tube on and with his arms extended straight ahead, the teacher should hold him with his hands high on the child's upper arms. Gradually, as the beginner gets used to the increased distance between himself and the instructor, the teacher slides his hold down the arms until finally he is merely holding the child's hands. As the distance between the two increases, the instructor must be careful to see that his student does not become tense. There must also be no excessive twisting of the child's torso or any other sign of overworking that might lead to a bad kicking action. From the hips up, the child should be almost totally relaxed and limp in the water.

The tube at this point is a "crutch" and eventually will be thrown away. In effect, it only replaces the instructor in part, allowing him to get farther away and in a better position to begin teaching the arm action combined with the kick. If the child lacked any support in mid-body at this point, he would start working harder to stay up and would be obliged to put his feet down more often in the shallows to rest. The bottom then would be a crutch.

In each lesson, the teacher should let his pupil put his feet down, walk around and play in the water, but during actual instruction, the tube is a far better aid than constant reliance on the bottom. With a tube, the child becomes accustomed to being *at ease in the correct prone position*, learning the correct kick action slowly and easily and earning for himself the all-important sense of balance that is necessary when he starts practicing the arm action.

Arm Action

Teaching the use of the arms in the crawl can be simple, provided the instructor understands a few subtleties that

18

are not readily apparent to the casual eye. In the crawl, the movement of the arms is essentially an alternating action; that is, the swimmer propels himself with first one arm and then the other. As one hand—let's say the right—*catches* hold of the water ahead of the swimmer and *presses* down and back against the water to propel him, the other hand is *recovering* forward out of the water. Then, when the left hand catches the water ahead of the swimmer and presses, the right hand is recovering out of the water.

During the catch and the press, each hand does move down and back with relation to the body, but the ideal, with relation to the water, is to have the hand hold one point in the water and thus propel the body past this fixed point.

At the start of the press under water, each hand should catch the water directly ahead of the swimmer. During the press, the whole arm, shoulder to fingertips, is straight but not rigidly stiff. Preferably, the fingers of the hand are together during the press, and it is important that the wrist be kept stiff enough so that the hand stays in line with the forearm.

A swimmer gets the most lift and power in the first part of the press, from the moment the hand has caught the water ahead until the arm and hand have traveled down and back slightly past the point where they are at right angles to the body. This "power zone" of the press then encompasses slightly more than half the total arc through which the arm and hand travel under water.

If the arm and hand are kept straight but not rigidly stiff during the press, then, as the swimmer starts to ease off pressure past the power zone, there will be a slight natural bending at the elbow as the hand comes up alongside the hip to start the recovery.

Right arm presses slowly,
left finishes recovery.

If you put on a face mask and stood directly in front of a good crawl swimmer, you would see that at the moment either hand is catching the water directly ahead of him, his shoulders are parallel to the water surface. Then, as the forward arm starts to press, you would see that the shoulder of this pressing arm dips slightly and the shoulder of the opposite arm is rising moderately, facilitating recovery of the opposite arm out of the water. At the start of the recovery, the elbow of the recovering arm is bent and relaxed,

20

so that the upper arm moving at the shoulder serves as a lever to carry the rest of the arm forward until the whole arm and hand are straight ahead to perform the catch and press.

The most important idea about the crawl stroke that the beginner can learn is that the hand does not try to *pull through* the water but *press against* it so that the body moves *through* the water.

Right arm speeds to begin recovery, left starts slow press.

When showing the learner the stroke, the teacher should first guide one arm through the cycle of catching, pressing and recovering, while holding the other arm on the surface straight ahead of the youngster. When the child has the feel of the action separately in each arm, the teacher should then move the child's arms in alternation. While the arm action takes place, the child kicks. Synchronization of arm and leg will come naturally, *provided the pupil continues kicking while learning to use the arms.*

Usually, a child who keeps kicking easily while practicing the arm action comes smoothly into a six-beat kick, which means that the feet, moving up and down, pass each other six times while the arms complete a full cycle.

It is important to remember that the child should keep

21

on kicking while practicing with the arms, so that he does not sacrifice one important action for the sake of acquiring another.

Right arm moves faster in recovery, left continues press.

The arm movement in the crawl is essentially, but not precisely, an alternate action. In the illustration, the arms are not exactly a half cycle apart at this moment. But, in actuality, each arm tends to catch up with the opposite arm during the recovery and then lag behind during the press. The reason is that while water is buoyant, air is not. A good crawl swimmer is like a ship with a constantly shifting ballast. Each part of his body that emerges from the water is a dead weight, a burden to the rest of him. Paradoxically, the more he can keep his body in the water, the higher the swimmer rides in the water.

As one arm and then the other comes out of the water to recover, the swimmer's weight shifts from side to side. Logically, then, it is desirable to speed up each arm during the recovery above water, where the arm is only a burden, and equally desirable to move the arm more slowly during the press under water, where the arm is serving the useful purpose of stabilizing, lifting and propelling the swimmer in the water. In the crawl, it is important to minimize the amount of the body that is out of the water at any time during the stroke cycle.

Right arm finishes recovery before starting catch, left finishes press. Arm positions now opposite to those shown on page 20.

All this becomes important when the proper way to breathe is taught. When the teacher is guiding the child's hands through the stroke, he need not worry much about the precise catch-up of each arm during the recovery. He need only direct the child's arms in approximate alternation through the proper course and emphasize that each hand must press gently and slowly rather than pull through the water.

Breathing Action

Breathing is the number-one bugaboo of incompetent swimmers. If the human head were weightless, breathing while swimming the crawl stroke would not be much of a problem. The casual swimmer would merely keep his head above water all the time and move along easily enough. A good swimmer who is well-conditioned can indeed go quite a distance carrying the burden of his head above water, but the average swimmer who tries it experiences soon afterward fatigue in the muscles of his back, neck and arms, as well as a distressing shortness of breath. As he tires, he must work harder and harder to hold his head up for air, and in working harder, he needs still more air. In no time at all, he is thrashing and struggling, played out and convinced that the water is a fit place only for supermen.

For a beginner, the final problem of the crawl stroke is to learn to get as much air as he needs in each breath, getting it as effortlessly as possible so he does not create a need for still more air. The basic principle that water is buoyant while air is not applies once again. Thus, when a beginner is moving slowly and easily through the water, the more he can keep all parts of his body, including the head, *under* the water, the higher and more effortlessly he will ride in the water. The higher he rides in the water, the more easily he will be able to get his mouth out of the water to get a breath. And the more easily he gets his mouth up for air, the less air he will need.

When he is not taking a breath, a good crawl swimmer keeps most of his head submerged, his face held comfortably straight ahead so the water breaks at about the hairline. As one arm, for example the left, catches and presses, the swimmer rolls slightly to the left side. The opposite shoulder, the right in this case, is riding higher, facilitating recovery of the right arm out of the water. Obviously, the moment when the right shoulder is riding high is a good time to take a breath on the right side, since the swimmer need only turn the face slightly more to the right to bring the mouth and nose above water level. The breath is taken quickly as the right arm—the arm on the breathing side—starts the recovery, and as the right arm continues forward,

24

completing the recovery, the face turns back down until it is again under water. The process of getting the mouth up for air, then, is a coordination of two movements: (1) the rotation of the whole body so that the shoulder on the breathing side is riding slightly higher, bringing the mouth part way to the surface on that side, and (2) a slight rotation of the head at the neck, to bring the mouth the rest of the way out of the water. The swimmer who does not rotate at the neck of necessity must roll the whole body more, and consequently a good bit of the shoulder will emerge—an unnecessary burden.

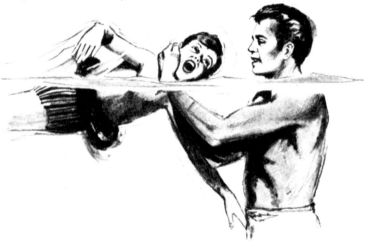

When the beginner is being taught the kick, he should practice exhaling and inhaling through both mouth and nose. Wearing the small tube around his waist for support, the child should now start kicking while the instructor takes his wrists and guides him through the correct arm action. The child's head is still above water, but as his left hand catches the water ahead, he should turn his face to the right side and exhale, then inhale through both nose and mouth.

Then, as the right arm comes forward to catch, his face is turned to the front. The teacher may guide the youngster vocally: "Turn, exhale, inhale, front." When the child gets the rhythm, the teacher removes his hands from his wrists, leaving only the small tube around the waist for support while the child kicks, strokes with his arms and, still holding his head above water, turns his face to the side and then back to the front, thus learning to harmonize the breathing rhythm with the arm movements.

The next project is to get the beginner used to putting his face under water, while at the same time holding his breath and opening his eyes under water.

For this experience, the neophyte should be taken into shallower water where he can stand. He still wears the tube during this part of the lesson. The teacher now takes the child's hands and has him push off the bottom and kick up to the surface until he floats facedown while holding his breath. When the pupil can keep this position for five seconds, he should kick up to the surface; but now, when level on the surface, he should use his arms and also practice the breathing action, turning the face up to exhale and inhale. The instructor still holds the child's hands as he kicks up to the prone position. Then he lets go and gently places one hand on either side of the child's face to guide him in coordinating head movement with arm action. When the coordination is good, the teacher removes his hands and lets the child practice supported only by the tube. For the present, to give better buoyancy, the child continues to hold his breath under water, both exhaling *and* inhaling when he has turned his face above water. As he improves, he will of his own accord start exhaling sooner, while his face is still under.

This is as far as a beginner can go on the road to successful swimming while using the tube for support. We now turn back and start over without the tube. At first, the child practices only kicking as he did at the very beginning, with the instructor's hands supporting his hips. The procedure now takes place in water that comes up to the teacher's neck, enabling him to reach out farther so that the child will have clearance on either side to start using his arms in harmony with the kick.

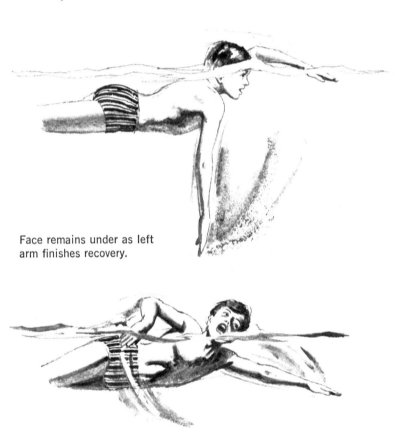

Face remains under as left arm finishes recovery.

Face is up for air, right arm starts recovery, left presses.

For a while after the tube is removed, when the youngster is kicking, using his arms and turning his face up and back in a correct breathing action, he will have the feeling of being heavier in the water. It is important that the pupil stay relaxed and not fight or work hard to offset the sinking feeling.

Gradually, as the teacher feels his young friend getting lighter and lighter, he lessens the upward pressure of his hands until finally he cannot feel the child's weight at all. Then the teacher drops his hands so that the beginner is actually going a stroke or two on his own. When the teacher pulls his hands away, he should back away from the child, but still keep his hands just below his body ready to apply gentle pressure again if he notices that the youngster is struggling too much.

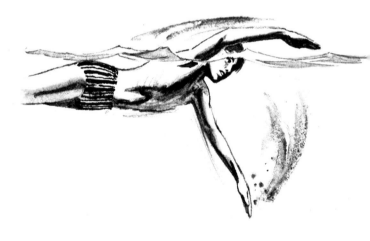

Face is back under as right arm finishes recovery.

When the child can do six or eight strokes in this manner, he is swimming. But he is not yet a swimmer.

THE BACKSTROKE

The crawl stroke is without question the best stroke for a child to know in order to use and enjoy the water safely. There are two other practical strokes commonly used today: (1) the backstroke and (2) the breaststroke. While the crawl serves well in most situations, there are very good reasons why every child should also be competent in the backstroke and the breaststroke.

The principal reason to know more than one of the practical strokes is simply that versatility means durability in the water. As he tires, any swimmer is apt to lose form and rhythm and, consequently, efficiency. Without a doubt, a swimmer suffers more than a runner from loss of form and rhythm, for the swimmer is literally surrounded by the medium through which he moves. As a tiring swimmer gets sloppy, he loses power and, worse than that, actually nullifies much of his force by incorrect actions that create resistance.

The crawl, the backstroke and the breaststroke all use virtually every muscle in the body, but each of these strokes uses the muscles differently. Thus, the versatile three-stroke swimmer, when going a distance, can change strokes and give his muscles, in a sense, some relief while he keeps moving. The versatile swimmer is more efficient, hence safer in the water.

There are, moreover, specific situations where the backstroke and breaststroke serve better than the crawl. Sometimes it is important for a swimmer to have a good look around while moving through the water. In such instances, both the backstroke and breaststroke are better than the crawl. The breaststroke is particularly valuable in rough water or in a brisk chop that can play hob with a crawl swimmer's rhythm as he tires. Wave riders burrowing under big, broken waves to reach the break line must use the breaststroke or some modification of it.

29

The backstroke is the logical second stroke to teach a child because it is essentially a crawl stroke executed on the back. The backstroke kick and the crawl kick are quite similar. In both strokes, too, the arms alternate, the swimmer presses and propels himself with one arm as he recovers the other arm forward out of the water.

The crawl and the backstroke may be taught together, and such mixing of instruction makes the learning process more interesting for the child. It is best not to start teaching the backstroke kick until the youngster has some command of the crawl kick, nor to teach the backstroke arm action until he has used the arms to some degree in the crawl. There are certain technicalities to the backstroke, and the good teacher should always explain these whys and wherefores to his charges. But it is best to keep such explanations fairly simple.

In one obvious respect, the backstroke is simpler for a beginner than the crawl. Because the pupil's face is out of water all the time, breathing is no great problem. To achieve fair competence on the back, the child needs only to coordinate two important actions, (1) the kick and (2) the arm stroke, and does not have to be concerned about movement of the head.

All things considered, however, the backstroke is not as easy for a beginner, nor as efficient for any swimmer, as the crawl. Beginners usually have trouble maintaining a good body position when they start learning on their back. Moreover, because of the design of the human body, anyone swimming the crawl gets a good, solid press with his arms moving straight down through the water. On his back, a swimmer must sweep his arms to the side, like oars.

Kick

In the backstroke, as in the crawl, first teach the beginner the kick, then add the arm stroke to it. When foot-deep water is available, present the kick action to the child as he lies in this shallows. He supports his upper body by reclining on his elbows. The kick, like the crawl kick, emanates from the hips, one leg lifting up as the other drops back down. As they move, the legs should be quite limp, somewhat relaxed at the knee, so that as each drops down it is fairly straight and as it lifts up there is a slight, natural flexing at the knee. The feet should be limp, as limp as can be —waggling loose as if the swimmer were trying to kick a shoe or slipper off the foot.

When they first try the backstroke kick, many children are inclined to kick too hard, creating a great splash instead of merely ruffling the surface with a gentler, more efficient action. Each foot should barely break the surface, and for a child of ten or younger, go no deeper than six or eight inches.

Here again, the basic rule applies: water is buoyant; air is not. Bringing the foot out of the water not only wastes energy, but also the sudden emergence of one foot in the unbuoyant air creates an unnecessary burden that destroys the all-important rhythm and balance, tending to drive the opposite foot too deep. When the opposite foot goes too deep, rather than propelling, it is creating resistance. Remember that, as in the crawl, the kick's prime value is not to propel, but to stabilize and to afford lift to the lower, less buoyant half of the body, so that the whole body lies

in a more horizontal, less resistant plane in the water.

Even though the pupil is not kicking too hard, nor bringing either foot too far out of the water or dropping it too deep, he is still liable to commit another error common to neophytes learning the crawl: pumping, or bicycling the legs. As in the crawl, this may be corrected by having the child stiffen the knee slightly while kicking.

When the teacher is first introducing the learner to the backstroke kick, if there is no good shallows available, he can demonstrate the idea of the kick on land. He holds the child's feet and guides his legs through the proper action while the pupil leans back on his elbows and reclines on the ground. The action should not be practiced too much on land, because the legs weigh far more out of water. To simulate the kick on land requires considerably more stiffening of the knee than would be the case during proper

kicking in the water, and the difficulty may be discouraging.

For most of the kicking practice, as in the crawl, the beginner should be taken out into deep water, chest-high, where he can easily be supported in the correct body position.

Because there is no breathing problem to complicate the matter, in the backstroke the instructor can begin to inculcate good body position while the child is practicing the kick. Because much of the lift afforded by the kicking action is at the feet, and because the upper body is more buoyant than the thighs and hips, beginners tend to sag

at the hips. Ideally, a backstroker lies fairly straight from the toes to the middle of the back, the upper back and shoulders curving up slightly, the chin tucked in a little so the head tilts slightly toward the feet.

Beginners should lie, not as they would on a hard board, but as they might on a mattress with a pillow under their head, their chin tucked and head tilted so they can see their toes. It should always be remembered that the lungs are built-in water wings, and if the youngsters will give a little thought to pressing down on these water wings, their hips consequently will stay up better.

While the pupil practices kicking, his head rests on the teacher's shoulder, or against his chest, depending on the depth of the water. The teacher gives support with both hands underneath and high on the child's hips, the heels of the teacher's hands actually in the small of the beginner's back. In water, with just a gentle pressure from the instructor's hands, a child will not sag at all. The pressure need only be gentle, never any more than the youngster requires to stay relaxed while kicking easily. Even though the child's kick looks good after a few tries, he should continue practicing the action until it is quite automatic, so that when he takes up the arm action, he can carry on the kick without much thought.

Arm Stroke

When a backstroker presses the water with his hand to propel himself, ideally the hand holds one spot in the water while the body slides past. The arm movements to be described are thus in relation to the body rather than to the water surrounding it.

If a good backstroker were superimposed on the face of a clock, with the head pointed to twelve o'clock and the feet to six, it would be noted that the right hand enters the water —or "catches" the water—at about seven minutes of twelve, and the left hand at seven minutes after twelve. As the hand catches, the palm is vertical, the outside edge of the hand (the edge along the little finger) entering the water first. The arm is straight, but the elbow not stiffly locked. From the catch through the press, until the hand ends up alongside the upper thigh, the arm does not travel in a shallow plane like the oar of a racing shell, but rather, arcs downward like an ordinary rowboat oar, angling about 30 degrees below the horizontal at the deepest point half-way through the arc.

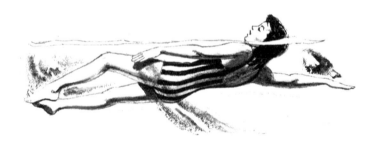

Right arm starts press, body rolls slightly to right.

Among topnotch backstrokers, arm actions vary a great deal. Some bend the arm a good bit as they finish the press, but for the beginner it is best to keep the arm fairly straight.

Some good backstrokers, to get the most out of each stroke, keep pressing, pushing against the water until the arm is virtually parallel to the body, hand along the thigh.

37

Any backstroker naturally gets the most power as the arm swings past the shoulder, when the hand is pressing at right angles to the line of travel. The beginner should be taught to start pressing easily from the catch until the arm passes through the midpoint of the arc, then slacken off, so that at the very end of the stroke the arm is virtually drifting in alongside the body.

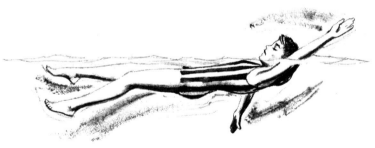

Right arm goes through power zone, body rides level.

During the press, as in the crawl, the hand should be flat, not cupped, the fingers together but not tense. Actually with the fingers spread, a swimmer gets about the same press on the water. There is one more significant flaw to watch for: some children tend to let the wrist go slack. The hand then bends back and slips through the water rather than pressing against it.

Left arm presses, body rolls to left.

During the recovery, as the arm comes out of the water alongside the thigh and moves forward beyond the swimmer's head to start another stroke, it should be kept straight, but here again, not stiff. On leaving the water at the start of the recovery, the hand is vertical, but during the recovery it should be turned slightly so that the palm faces the feet.

Left arm eases, right finishes recovery.

By trying this turn of the palm on land, it will be apparent that if the palm is toward the feet, the rotation of the arm at the shoulder during the recovery will put the palm again vertical, with the outside edge of the hand once more entering the water first on the next stroke. To recover the arm, the pupil should not lift it vertically over the body, but out, away from the body at a slight angle. This prevents water from sloshing down into the face and, more important, brings the arm correctly to the entry position at "seven minutes of and seven minutes after."

In the backstroke, as in the crawl, there is necessarily some body roll, a roll to the side of the arm that is at the moment pressing. This puts the opposite shoulder slightly higher, facilitating recovery of the opposite arm. Ideally, the whole body should be rolling cleanly, as if impaled on a spit. In the beginner, it is necessary to make sure that the roll is not excessive, not creating too much unnecessary resistance or destroying the all-important rhythm of the stroke.

The beginner can get a mechanical idea of the stroke by going through it while lying on a bench on land, but the real feel of it can come only with the support and resistance afforded by water. For actual practice, the pupil should again be taken into shoulder-high waters and supported as before when he first practiced kicking. The teacher then gradually slips his hands up the child's back and finally takes hold gently on the back of his upper arms, just below the armpits. Then, as the child continues kicking easily, the instructor guides his arms alternately through the stroke.

The youngster is not apt to have much sense of buoyancy nor feel at ease until he acquires rhythm and, consequently, some power to carry himself along. If necessary to keep him at ease, a small tube—such as the one used in teaching the crawl—may be inflated just enough to give natural support and placed around the child's waist. Eventually, when the child begins to get the feel of the arm action, the teacher may release his grip on the upper arms and let the beginner go it alone, without the tube and with only the teacher's hands under the back. When the pupil gains confidence in his own buoyancy, the instructor gradually eases the pressure of his hands underneath, until finally the child is backstroking completely on his own.

THE BREASTSTROKE

Though the crawl, because of its greater efficiency, is broadly recognized as *the* basic stroke, the breaststroke remains a valuable part of the average swimmer's repertoire.

Though it is far less efficient than the crawl, the breaststroke is essentially an easy stroke, very conducive to relaxation. A beginner can commit several errors and still move along inefficiently but very easily, almost restfully.

It is the basic law of swimming—that water is buoyant, while air is not—which makes the breaststroke com-

paratively restful. In both the crawl and backstroke, because he must recover first one arm and then the other through unbuoyant air—and in the crawl, turn the head to one side for air—a swimmer is like a ship with a constantly shifting ballast. The breaststroke affords considerably more stability and flotation. For one thing, in the breaststroke the arms are never out of water, even on the recovery. The head is the only part of the body ever out of water, and even at that, to take air, the head is lifted straight to the front, not out of line to the side, as in the crawl. For another thing, in contrast to the alternating and essentially vertical action of arms and legs in the crawl, in the breaststroke the arms move in unison and the legs in unison through a somewhat horizontal plane, further improving the swimmer's stability.

The underwater recovery of the arms and legs that contributes so much to the swimmer's flotation also, unfortunately, makes the breaststroke inefficient. By recovering under water, all four of the swimmer's limbs are to some extent opposing his forward progress for part of each cycle. Because of this, the all-important lesson, and the hardest for a beginner to learn, is timing—sneaking the recovery of the arms and legs into the cycle so that they impede forward progress the least.

Kick

As in the crawl and the backstroke, the pupil must first practice the kick. The breaststroke kick is essentially a thrusting action. The beginner must first recover his legs forward from the extended position before he can kick.

In the recovery, the child flexes at the hips and knees and, keeping his heels fairly close together, draws his feet forward until, at the completion of the recovery, his upper and lower legs form a diamond. The feet, legs and knees are in much the same position they would assume if he had stopped midway while doing a deep knee bend with his knees spread about eighteen inches apart. To start the kick, the beginner, presses the soles of his feet flat against the water, then thrusts his legs back until they are again straight but with his feet apart (for a nine-year-old child, about two feet apart). Finally, he brings his extended legs back together, in effect closing a wedge that squeezes the water and tends to propel him forward. Before beginning the next recovery, he glides for an instant on the momentum of the kick. While the kick can be divided mechanically into four parts—(1) a recovery forward, (2) a thrust back, (3) a squeeze together and (4) a glide—from the recovery through the squeeze, the action should flow without interruption. There is never any pause except for the glide between the squeeze and the recovery.

The teacher should first show the youngster the mechanics of the kick on land, guiding his legs through the action and then having him try it, unassisted, by sitting on the ground and leaning back supporting his upper body on his elbows. For such practice, logically, the pupil should lie prone, but since on the recovery the knees actually come up somewhat underneath the body, the correct prone position is impossible when the kick is first tried on land.

As in other strokes, the real practice of the kick is done in water. Since the breaststroke is now taught as a secondary stroke to swimmers who already have learned the fundamentals of the crawl and are at ease in the water, it is not necessary to hold the child while he practices, but rather, let him support his upper body on a kickboard. A pine board, about two inches thick, ten or twelve inches wide and two feet long, will do. When the pupil holds a board of this sort out at arm's length, the body is correctly level in the water and the board offers resistance that best simulates actual swimming. As in the other strokes, he should practice kicking until the action is virtually automatic, so he can next concentrate on the arm action without giving the legs much thought.

Arm Stroke

1

Between strokes, swimmer lies streamlined while she glides through water, her arms extended ahead and legs in line to the rear, creating little resistance.

2

To propel herself, swimmer first presses her arms out and back, at the same time lifting her face to take a breath. While she presses with her arms, her legs remain extended so they do not impede her forward progress.

Mechanically, the movement of the arms in the breaststroke, like the kicks, is a four-part action. The correct arm action is shown in the sequence above. In drawing 1, the arms are extended to the front, as if the young swimmer just dived into the water. To propel herself, she simply presses outward and back in an arc, shown in drawing 2. During the press, she keeps her arms straight but not rigid. The arms do not sweep back in a shallow, horizontal plane, but rather, travel somewhat downward as they move back. At the finish of the press, when the hands are a little past the line of the shoulder, the arms are angling down about 30 degrees below horizontal.

3

4

In the recovery, swimmer flexes at the hips and knees to draw feet forward. While doing this, she starts arm recovery by dropping elbows and sliding forearms inward until her hands are in front of her face, palms down.

The kick starts as swimmer thrusts her feet back vigorously until her legs are extended and her feet about two feet apart. As she begins to kick in this manner, she is completing the recovery of her arms by sliding them straight ahead of her.

There are two parts to the recovery of the arms in the breaststroke. First, by flexing her shoulders and elbows, the child tucks her upper arms in fairly close to the body, at the same time sliding her hands in together, as in drawing 3. As she does this, the palms of her hands face the bottom so they create less resistance as they slip laterally through the water. In the second part of the recovery, she thrusts her arms forward (drawing 4). When her arms are fully extended, her hands together directly ahead of her (drawing 5),

Finishing stroke, swimmer has squeezed her extended legs together again and glides for a moment before starting next stroke.

she is ready to start the next press. Before pressing again, however, there is a pause to glide. The pause of the arms is not as pronounced as that of the legs—the actual duration depends largely on the pace that the swimmer is setting. A good swimmer, moving very easily and very slowly, will glide with arms and legs extended for as long as a second.

46

If each of the parts of the arm action coincided exactly with one part of the kick, the breaststroke would indeed be simple. But the parts do not coincide, and most beginners need to practice kick and arm stroke together a good bit to get the correct timing down reasonably well. In drawing 2, when the pupil presses with her arms, her legs are still extended, quite logically slipping through the water, offering as little resistance as possible while she propels herself with her arms. As she finishes pressing and brings her arms in toward her body, she is recovering her legs, drawing her feet forward. Then, as she executes the last part of the arm recovery, extending her arms to the front, she has thrust back with her feet and is squeezing her extended legs together. Finally, with both arms and legs extended and together, she pauses again, gliding before repeating the cycle.

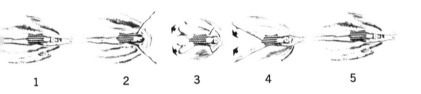

| 1 | 2 | 3 | 4 | 5 |

The beginner can be taught the mechanics of the arm action on land, but proper coordination of arms and legs will only come with practice in the water. Since the timing is rather tricky, it is best for the pupil to concentrate on arms and legs without incorporating the action of the head.

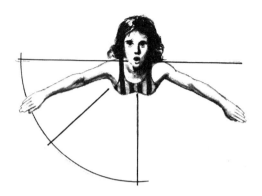

A child who is quite buoyant and completely at ease in the water can practice using his arms and legs, holding his head out of water all the time, without any support from the instructor. If the head is up, the feet will tend to ride a bit low, but usually not so low as to spoil the rhythm or to keep the child from concentrating on the job at hand.

However, if he seems tense and must work too hard to maintain a good body position, he should start practicing coordination of arms and legs with an inflated tube around his waist. The tube's resistance, true, somewhat nullifies the streamlining of the body that is so important during the glide, but this unnatural resistance is a worthwhile price to pay at the start to keep the child relaxed while he concentrates on timing.

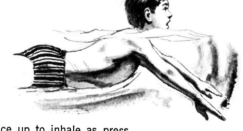

Swimmer tilts face up to inhale as press of arms lifts body.

Swimmer exhales under water as arms begin recovery.

Once a swimmer gets arms and legs working fairly well, the head action is quite simple. At the end of the glide, as the arms start to press, the face is tilted up until the mouth is just clear of the water. The breath is taken while the arms press. Then, when the arms start to recover in toward the body, the face is turned back down and the swimmer exhales as the hands are thrust forward. When the face is submerged, it is not straight down but tilted slightly forward so that, as in the crawl, the waterline is about mid-forehead.

Swimmer finishes exhaling during glide between strokes.

Even when the beginner is combining head action with the stroke and kick, a tube may be used if he tends to work too hard or too fast. The tube will enable him to get a good feel of the rhythm, which is so important in this stroke, where timing and streamlining are of the essence.

Part 2
Diving

THE DIVER

If swimming can be likened to running, then diving may perhaps be compared to gymnastics. Yet it is more than just a wholesome exercise that tests both the body and the brain. At its best, it approaches an athletic art form, a pursuit of beauty for beauty's sake. And from the amateurs to the Olympic medalists, there is something about being a diver that immediately sets them apart from the crowd.

For the novice, as in any sport, the keys to success are continued hard work and respect for fundamentals. While beginning divers can teach themselves many fundamentals, they do need a certain amount of on-the-spot attention, if not from a master of the art, at least from someone with a good grasp of the fundamentals. Until a diver acquires "feel" through experience, he must count heavily on his coach or fellow divers to evaluate his dives.

Any dive—the simplest or the most difficult—is in essence a beautiful flow, a blending of fast actions into a single flowing movement of seemingly effortless elegance and grace. Much of the fundamental action of a simple forward dive is of equal importance in the execution of a complicated double-twisting one and a half somersault. When you take your first step toward learning the simplest dives, you are quite literally also starting your conquest of the most difficult diving feats.

You need not be the absolute master of one dive before trying others of greater degree of difficulty, so long as you continue to dedicate yourself to perfection of the fundamentals, constantly bearing in mind that you can never do hard dives consistently until you have the easier ones well under control.

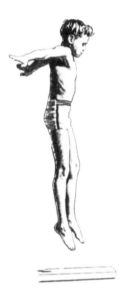

Until you have achieved reasonable competence, confine your practice to the standard one-meter board—the low board, as it is called. Springboards vary quite a bit. Some are slow and pliant; some are fast and stiff. Most have an adjustable fulcrum, allowing you to change the character of the board to suit your weight, style and the particular dive you are trying.

Most boards are properly installed parallel to the water so that, when the board is flexed downward and starts to spring back up, you are actually propelled slightly outward away from the board.

In the beginning, you will not have good control of your body, and on the first dives will tend to cast yourself out too far or to either side. Accordingly, to be safe, you should have at least ten feet of water not only under the correct entry spot, but also extending at least three feet in back of the end of the board, eight feet to either side and ten feet to the front of the board.

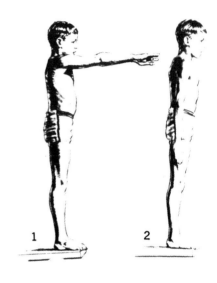

STANDING FRONT JUMP

The purpose of a springboard obviously is to afford elevation sufficient to execute the dive successfully. Your first job is to learn a synchronized action of the arms and legs that you will use—with slight modification—to get lift from the board on every dive you try.

To begin, take a standing position at the end of the board, then spring into the air and enter the water feet first. (See

the first sequence of drawings.) You are executing a "standing front jump," and by practicing it you begin learning not only the critical synchronization of arms and legs to gain lift but also several other important fundamentals.

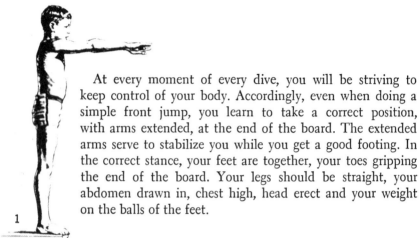

At every moment of every dive, you will be striving to keep control of your body. Accordingly, even when doing a simple front jump, you learn to take a correct position, with arms extended, at the end of the board. The extended arms serve to stabilize you while you get a good footing. In the correct stance, your feet are together, your toes gripping the end of the board. Your legs should be straight, your abdomen drawn in, chest high, head erect and your weight on the balls of the feet.

When you feel stable in this position, then lower your arms to the sides, being careful to preserve the trim, erect posture; be careful also that the shift of the weight of your arms from in front of you to your sides does not put your whole weight back on your heels.

56

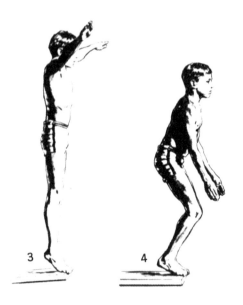

It is from the position shown in drawing 2 that you actually start the arm and leg action to get lift from the board. Briskly sweep the arms upward and slightly forward, simultaneously straightening your ankles so that you rise up on the balls of your feet.

Then, with increasing speed, sweep the arms slightly back and downward in an arc, at the same time bending the knees and flexing the ankles until the heels are back down flat on the board. As the heels come back down on the board, the downsweeping arms continue in an arc, and with no hesitation, start traveling back up. It is primarily this sudden change in direction by the arms that exerts pressure downward on the board. As the board is depressed, carry the arms on up, over your head and slightly in front of it, at the same time, with as much force as you can control, driving off the board with your legs and feet.

When the arm sweep and leg drive carry you to maximum height, you have completed the important lesson of synchronization, but there are other fundamental actions that you can begin learning during the simple straight drop down into the water. At maximum height, bring your arms down to the side horizontal position, the crucifix position shown in drawing 6. In this position, the arms have a stabilizing effect.

Just before you hit the water when executing a standing front jump, drop your arms smartly to your sides to effect a clean, almost splashless entry.

When you first do a standing front jump, do not push too hard trying for maximum height, but rather, use only as much force as you can control while learning the proper synchronization of the arms and legs.

From a standing position, not even the best divers get enough height to make a simple forward dive look its best. Thus, take a series of steps culminating in one high bounding step called the "hurdle," and then, with feet together, bring your whole weight down on the end of the board.

6

7

1   2   3   4

5   6   7   8

Approach and hurdle with forward dive, layout position.

BOARD ACTION

The complete action of a forward dive is done in the layout position (the "swan dive," as it is popularly known).

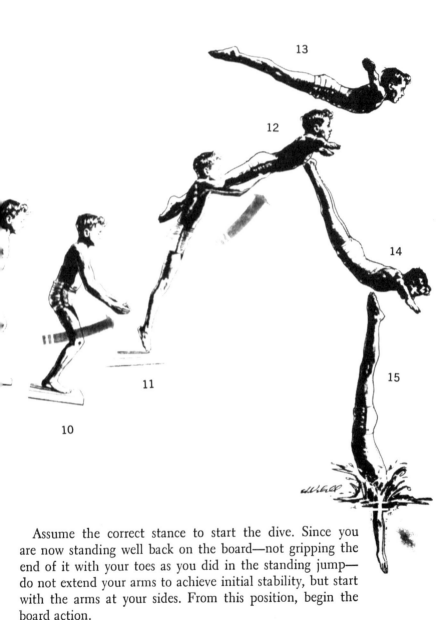

13

12

14

10

11

15

Assume the correct stance to start the dive. Since you are now standing well back on the board—not gripping the end of it with your toes as you did in the standing jump—do not extend your arms to achieve initial stability, but start with the arms at your sides. From this position, begin the board action.

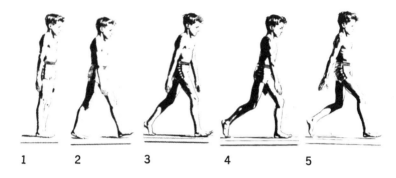

1   2   3   4   5

In drawings 2 through 5, a series of steps most commonly known as the "approach" is demonstrated. Most divers use a three-step approach, but in the beginning, use four steps. Each step is slightly longer than the preceding one, and with each, increase the tempo until in the final step (drawing 5), break almost into a run. Throughout this approach, maintain a trim posture, head fairly erect, lowered only enough to allow you to keep your eyes on the end of the board. The arms are held fairly straight but not stiff, the swing of each arm a trifle restrained but still in normal rhythm with the steps.

It is only as you bring your right leg forward to complete the fourth step (drawing 5) that you alter the arm rhythm a bit. The left arm, which would normally swing forward with the advance of the right leg, lags slightly behind, so it can then swing forward in unison with the right arm as you begin (drawing 6) the most important single element of the board action, the hurdle.

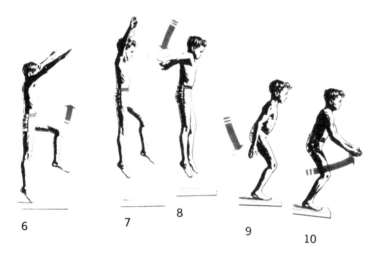

6   7   8   9   10

To execute the all-important hurdle, as your right foot comes down on the board to complete the last step of the approach, instead of bringing the left leg forward for another normal step, lift the left knee high, at the same time driving hard off the board with your right leg and sweeping the arms forward and upward (drawing 6). This unified effort of arms and legs carries you well off the board (drawing 7). As you rise to maximum height—the peak of the hurdle—bring your two legs together and, for stability, lower the arms to the side horizontal position. As you drop back down, the arms are out to the side, the legs are straight, toes reaching for the board (drawing 8).

After dropping down to the end of the board (drawings 9 through 11), forcefully use your arms and legs to press the board and depart from it as you did in the standing front jump, only now, with the whole weight of your body behind you, the board is depressed much farther and you are able to give yourself a greater lift into the air.

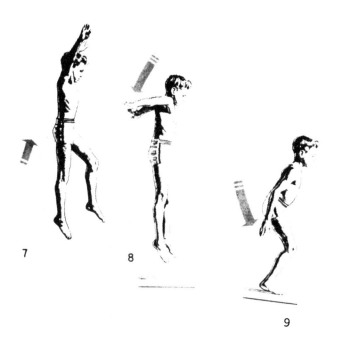

7   8

9

To practice the board action, you must first determine
which leg you will use to drive yourself up into the all-
important hurdle. On any level surface, try taking a step
and jumping off your right leg as you bring the left through
and lift the left knee high. Then do the same thing, revers-
ing legs, and settle on the one that feels most natural for
you to use consistently.

In the hurdle, you should try for height—good *balanced*
height. Never apply more force than you can control. Maintaining balance and control are far more difficult—and far
more critical—in the hurdle than in the simpler press and
lift from the standing position. The timing, too, is more

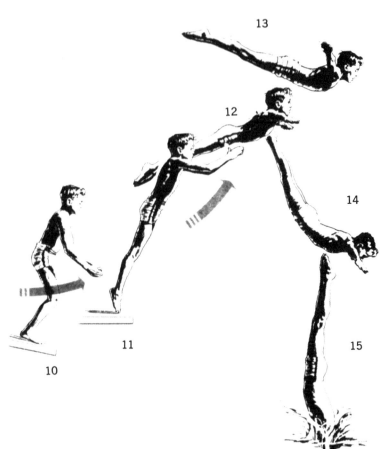

critical. When you come down to the end of the board from a hurdle, you are blending three forces: (1) the descending weight of your body, (2) the sweep of the arms and (3) the press of the legs. If the timing of any one of these forces is off, it nullifies the effect of the others.

The essential drive of the hurdle is virtually straight up. It is principally the momentum of the approach steps that carries the body forward to the end of the board. The breadth of the hurdle (the distance from last approach step to the end of the board) varies from diver to diver. Consistency is the important thing. The board is a lever. To get the most from it, you must land close to the end.

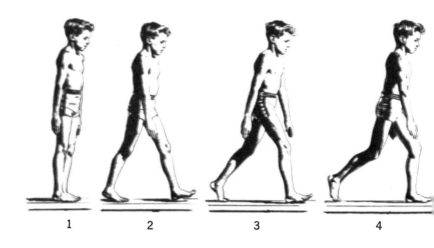

1 2 3 4

Before actually going onto a board, you should check your consistency on the ground. Merely take your first step from a fixed mark and have your coach, or a friend, spot each step, particularly the conclusion of the hurdle, where both feet come down as if to press the end of the board. When you can regularly hit within four or five inches of one spot, you are ready to try the approach and hurdle on the board.

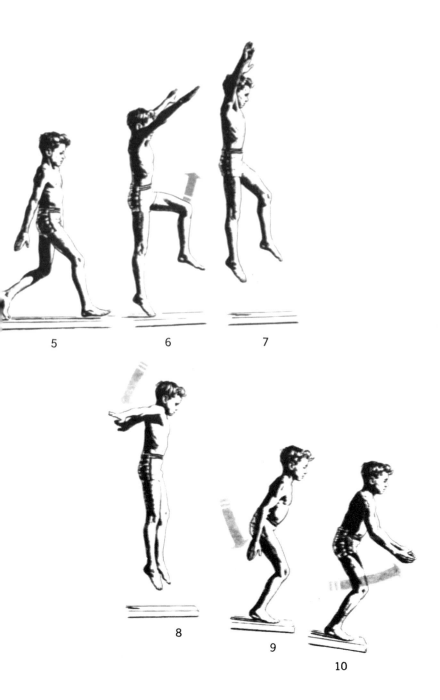

5   6   7

8

9

10

When you first practice on the board, for safety, as well as to maintain confidence and control, you should try a one-step approach and hurdle, finishing off with the front jump that you have already learned, rather than the forward swan dive. It's important that you practice this way at first.

You may have already gone headfirst off springboards, but if you tried a headfirst dive now, after concentrating as you have on the vertical action of the hurdle, you just

might get a slight backward lean, a backward cast, and come down, if not on the board, then unnervingly close to it. When you have confidence and control of a three-step approach and hurdle culminating in a front jump, you are ready to learn a headfirst dive.

FRONT HEADER

At this point, return to the basic standing position on the end of the board, except now you will culminate the press of the board and the lift up in a "front header." Your departure from the board is quite similar to that in the front jump, but this time you must cast yourself slightly more out away from the board, stretching the arms overhead, your head tilted only slightly back from the straight line of the body. Your legs should be straight, your toes pointed and, most important, the abdomen muscles contracted. With every muscle, virtually, try to keep the whole body in a straight line so that the drive from the board will carry the legs on up to a point slightly above the maximum achieved by the torso and the head. As you start to drop down from the top of the dive, lower your head until it is in line with the rest of your body—as you drop, stretch as hard as you can, reaching for the water with the whole streamlined body.

It looks easy, but it takes some doing. Concentrate on trying to bring the legs up fast. Constantly bear in mind that, since you are trying to keep the body straight at all times, you are dependent largely on the movement of the head to control the dive. Do not lift the head too far back at the top of the dive, creating an exaggerated arch of the body. It robs you of height, spoils the true expression of the dive and only makes it harder for you to get around to a vertical entry without bending in the middle.

Since a prime object of this dive is to maintain a straight body throughout, it is difficult to bring this dive into the water very close to the board. Try to enter from four to six feet out from the end of the board. On your entry—and this is important for all dives—do not think of the water surface as your target. It is merely a curtain. Concentrate on reaching for the bottom, "stretching the dive down."

SWAN DIVE

All the principles and movements of the front header apply to the forward "swan" dive, with one marked exception. In the front header, the arms are kept virtually straight ahead all the time, while in the forward swan dive, as you drive toward the top of the dive, the arms are carried out to the side horizontal position, held there through the top of the dive to give it expression and then briskly brought back in front of the head the instant before you stretch for the vertical entry into the water. This difference at the top of the dive enforces a slight variation as you depart from

72

the board. In the layout dive, as you drive upward, do not sweep the arms up until they are almost overhead, but sweep them up only a little past right angles with the main axis of the body. From this position, the arms are then simply and gracefully spread to the side horizontal position as you carry the dive to the top of the layout sequence.

The whole art of diving is built around three basic body positions: (1) the layout, (2) the pike and (3) the tuck. In carrying your body straight, with arms in the side horizontal position in the forward swan dive, you were using the layout position.

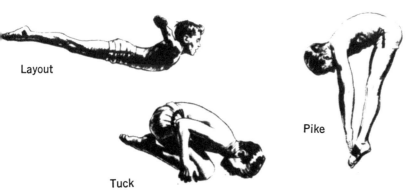

Layout

Tuck

Pike

FORWARD PIKE

The "forward pike," or "front jackknife," is a dive in which the pike is essentially a compact triangle, the legs, feet and pointed toes forming the longest side, and the upper body and arms forming the other two sides. For esthetic reasons, as well as to give you optimum control in complex dives, the pike should always be as compact as possible.

In the forward pike, the starting position, the approach, the hurdle and press of the board are identical to those of the forward dive, layout position.

The arms are never carried in the side horizontal position. Do not merely sweep your arms up slightly above head level as you did in the forward layout dive, but instead, sweep them well above your head as you did in the standing front jump. The reasons for this are simple: in the forward pike, you do not have to concern yourself with maintaining a straight body position while the drive from the board carries your feet and legs up higher than your head. As you near the top of the dive, you quite literally turn a sharp corner, so that, at the very top of the dive, the upper part of your body is already heading downward. Sweep up hard with your arms because your principal concern with this dive is getting good, controlled height, so that at the very top of the dive, your hips have carried up as high as your head was just an instant before.

If in forming the pike you had carried your legs too far forward to make contact with your hands, the center of balance would have been back, making it hard to get around to effect a decent, vertical entry.

1

2

3

4

5

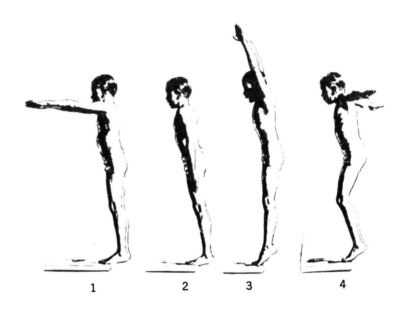

1   2   3   4

BACK DIVE LAYOUT

In this dive, you start with your back to the water and continue backward through the whole flight until you drop straight down for the entry. In a back dive, obviously, an approach and hurdle are impossible. You can only start at the end of the board. To gather lift from the board, you must rely solely on the synchronization of arms and legs that you learned in the standing front jump.

Before you try the correct mechanics of the simple "back dive layout", you must cope with a more fundamental problem. To go from an upright position to an upside-down

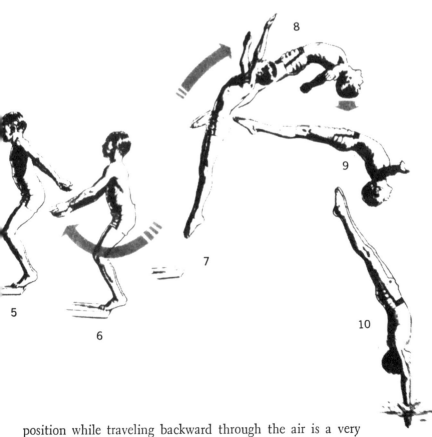

5 6 7 8 9 10

position while traveling backward through the air is a very unnatural act. Our fundamental instinct of self-preservation resists it. From a one-meter springboard, even if you land squarely on your back, it is almost impossible to hurt yourself. The worst you suffer is a sharp sting of the flesh, and even this can be avoided by wearing a T-shirt. But regardless of how confident you are that it is a safe act, if you try the whole mechanics of the dive right from the start, something inside of you is apt to rebel.

In the flight, you suddenly find yourself twisting your head or upper body to convert the backward movement into a more natural forward action. You must, in brief, first learn to dominate your basic instinct. To do this, have an experienced companion help you.

Standing front jump

Back dive

The initial stance is the same stabilizing position, with arms extended in front, that was assumed in the jump sequence demonstrating the standing front jump. But now, of course, you face the butt end of the board, your back to the water. Only your toes and the balls of your feet are on the board.

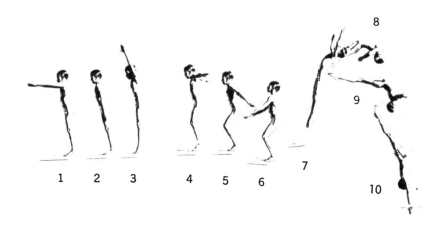

The balls of the feet are about a half an inch to an inch apart, but your heels extending beyond the end of the board are pressed together, enhancing your stability. When you feel that you are stable and that your footing is secure, extend your arms upward, overhead, while the teacher, or companion, holds you. Arch your back, bend your head back, stretching as if trying to see the water beyond you.

Then, just as you feel your balance carrying you off the board, bend your knees slightly, and the board moves downward with the balls of your feet. With no hesitation at all, straighten knees and ankles and drive up and backward away from the board, continuing to stretch back with your head, arms and shoulders, seeking the water below.

You cannot, of course, get good height until you are combining an arm swing to do the dive correctly. When you practice the full mechanics of this dive, one of your first concerns should be to effect a correct position of the upper body during the press and lift from the board.

In executing the standing front jump, carry your upper body at a slight forward angle. Even if you were to accentuate this forward lean more in the standing front jump, it would merely mean that you would cast yourself slightly farther away from the board, sacrificing height, but otherwise barely affecting your completion of the dive with a vertical entry. The angle of the upper body during the press and lift into a back dive is far more critical. You can err in

Standing front jump

Forward body lean

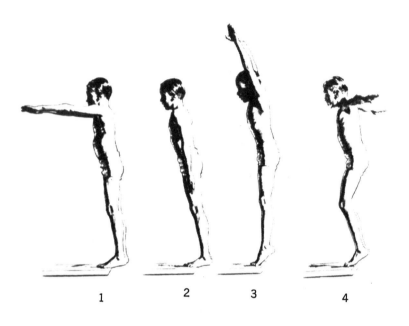

either direction. As in drawing 1, you are in the starting position. The arms drop to the sides with a lowering of the heels (drawing 2). You have, as in the standing front jump, lifted your arms and raised up on the balls of your feet (drawing 3). Then, as you sweep the arms down and flex your knees, you are ever so slightly off balance backward, but your upper body is fairly erect (drawing 4), somewhat like the middle of a deep knee bend—and for the average

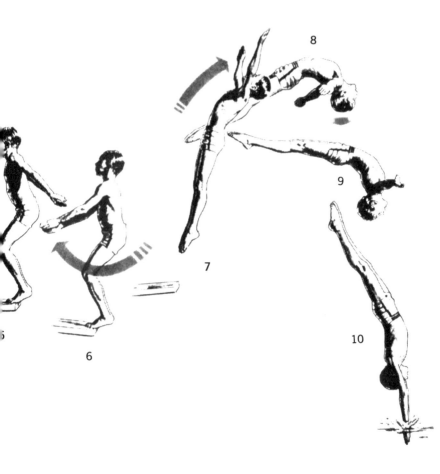

person, at this moment it is a natural tendency to lean slightly forward. If you lean forward, toward the board, then naturally you will tend to drive up but not sufficiently backward away from the board. You will have a hard time getting around and, worse, will come too close to the board. On the other hand, if you should lean too far back, your upper body angling away from the board, you tend to cast yourself too far out, losing height.

3   4   5   6

To achieve reasonable proficiency in this dive, you must unlearn part of the technique you just used in doing an intermediate back dive, starting with arms extended over your head. In the intermediate dive, with arms overhead, you could not get much height and, accordingly, you were obliged to arch backward rather severely from the start, to be sure of getting around. Now, as you try the correct back dive, sweeping your arms in concert with your leg action, concentrate more on carrying the body fairly straight as you drive up and backward. Then, at the top of the dive, as you spread your arms to the side horizontal position, bring the head back and throw the chest up, effecting an arch. The

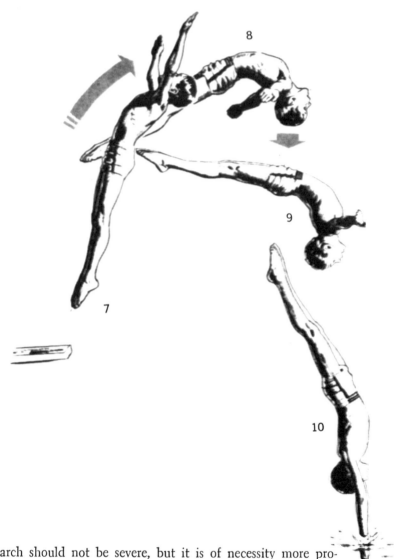

arch should not be severe, but it is of necessity more pronounced than that at the top of the forward dive, layout
position. As the head goes back at the top of the dive, look
for the water; then, as you drop for the entry, stretch the
whole body out, and reach with the whole body for the
water.

INWARD PIKE

In this dive, you start by taking the same stance as in the back dive, layout position. In your initial drive from the board, you are impelling yourself backward, but the actions of the dive are similar to those of the forward group. Since you are bringing your head and body in toward the board as you drop out of an inward dive, your entry is quite close to the board—three feet at most. First practice the takeoff by finishing with a simple foot-first entry—in other words, practice a standing back jump. For the greatest safety, first stand on one corner of the board, driving up and diagonally out from the corner of the board. When you are getting good, consistent clearance, then try the same standing back jump from the correct position in the center of the end of the board.

Next, go back to the corner of the board, and driving up and diagonally out as before, practice an intermediate sort of "inward pike." For this, take the regular back dive stance, but hold your extended arms straight overhead. Using only the drive you get from flexing knees and ankles, drive up and diagonally away from the board, then bend down for your toes to form a pike as you did in the forward dive, pike position. When your clearance is consistently good from the corner of the board, practice next this intermediate inward pike from the center of the end of the board.

1

2

After that, you are ready to try the whole correct mechanics of the dive. In this dive, as in the back dive layout, you must concentrate on driving up and out from the board, being careful to maintain the nearly vertical angle of the upper body as you press the board and drive off it. The action of the arms and legs to get lift from the board is practically the same as for the back dive.

Once your drive from the board carries you toward the top of the dive, you are going through actions virtually identical to those of the forward pike dive.

Naturally, since you do not have the advantage of a hurdle in this inward pike, you cannot get as much height and, accordingly, will have a harder time setting up a good compact pike at the top and then dropping out of it for a good entry.

FORWARD DIVE, HALF TWIST

The "forward dive," layout, with "half twist" is the simplest dive in what is called the twisting group. In diving, the word "twist" denotes one full rotation of the body on its long axis. Doing a half twist in a forward dive, then, means that while you leave the board facing forward, at the entry you will have rotated a half turn and will enter as you did when completing a back dive.

90

The twisting action is a continuous movement starting before the top of the dive and carrying through it. At the top of the dive, you have completed one half of your half twist and are, at this moment, in what may be called a "side swan position."

You are departing from the board as if doing a plain forward dive, but as you spread your arms to the side horizontal position, start your twist to the right. Set this twist

in motion by stretching your right arm downward, rolling your right shoulder so that it holds alignment with the arm. It is important that you do not rotate your head excessively but merely turn it in alignment with the shoulder, turning only as it rotates. As the legs are rising, and through the top of the dive, the stomach muscles must be sucked in taut to keep the body straight through the side swan position. As you start to drop from the top of the dive, continue ro-

tation of body to the right, now also stretching the opposite arm and shoulder in the opposite direction to bring the dive around a full half turn. Do not think at any moment of converting a forward dive into a back dive, but rather, consider your whole flight to be like that of a plane descending abruptly while banking sharply. And it is only after the full half turn has been achieved that you stretch your arms out ahead for the entry.

In twists, you can practice to the left or to the right, at your option. Regardless of direction, twisting is at first hard for the beginner to control. From the start in the half twist, you will have to resist the inclination to overtwist, to rotate the head excessively and throw the dive off. The important effort should be to learn to "set" the dive in the side swan position before continuing rotation for the vertical entry.